More Love Than Pressure

Kori Doty

BookLeaf Publishing

India | USA | UK

Presentation by *BookLeaf Publishing*

Web: www.bookleafpub.com

E-mail: info@bookleafpub.com

ISBN: 9789358314359

First edition 2023

DEDICATION

May these words and the sentiments that channeled them meet you when and where you need them.

ACKNOWLEDGEMENT

Big appreciations to my polycules, the sisterhood of the fist and the circle jerk of care. These poems were written on the land of the Lekwungan and WSANEC people in what is colonially known as Victoria BC.

more love than pressure

Where are we going to watch cartoons?
She asks from a partial consciousness
head on my chest.
My body shudders in silent tears
Contemplating the implications
Her body shudders in precarious attempts to find
comfort
Morphine itch
Enlarged liver pressure
The art and love of many more years trying to
get out
The body has been warned that its on it last
Get out while you can
Not me. I'm here. Not going anywhere
Don't want to let go
May need to, as not to wet the bed
Hold out a bit longer
There's more love than pressure

Hollow Resonance

In conversation
My brain to my body
My body to yours
My breakfast to my body
My body to the land
The land to my breakfast

Façades on sale
Offering shallow replications
Of
Profound ancient truths
Resonant beats
Big drums played by 8 bit midis
Depth probes come back hollow

Echoes rattle
Elephant graveyard melodies
Tinkled out on toy pianos

Heartbreaker

Breaking the hard news
Breaking hearts. Try to do
it gently. You can't

Hard news breaks hearts hard
The gentleness is still love
Destruction and love

Months not years she gets
Baby girl is on her way
Fifty wonderful

Cornocopia

Long tables
Rich with bounty
All the colours
Bright red tomatoes and radishes dot the salad
Orange yams and squashes steam in their glass
dishes
Yellow, golden brown skin glistening on a roast
bird,
belly of a beast, basted, brown
toasty soft buns baked fresh
Green salads and braised bacon greens
Blue and purple await us in a pie and crisp,
resting before being served a la mode
Looking across it all into the eyes of our lovers
As they look to theirs
A web

Slow Implosion

Sleeping upright
At least you are sleeping
Missing spoons
Modified now with padded layers
Holding your body together
With pillows. Strategically placed
The slowest implosion

I remember watching videos of Las Vegas Hotel
implosions.
Controlled, dramatic demolition.
Standing one moment. Dust and rubble the next.
Then the world trade center.
Watched those towers fall over and over.
That news story that embeds itself at a crucial
coming of age.
Do you remember watching the wall come
down?

Success in cancer treatment; a controlled
demolition
In part performative, while being edge play of
the nth degree
Political, absolutely. Politicizing? Between
treatment and side effects it's a wonder anyone

comes up for air let alone pen a great memoir or
complete a big opus.
But you will try
Not finished here yet
This is a deconstruction more than a demolition
Same ultimate result for those left behind
More clues and presents and treasures
In exchange for
More nausea, fullness, irregular spit, sweat, pee
and poo, aches, numbness, neuropathy
We aren't going to over sell it… but this is what
we can offer
Let go of everything you know. In your head and
your heart and your body.
Surrender
Spin the wheel
You could get lucky
For a while
Until you don't
You can play as long as you want
But there's pretty much the one game in town for
all this
Another round?

For now my sweet
I pray for sleep
That the pain lets you sleep
That the sleep takes you places
Where the things you worry about are alleviated

And your body feels peace
To keep getting more days
Or to find peace beyond your body
The body propped up by pillows
Beautiful and tender
And so very badly wanting to keep living

Desire dances

Direct answers require direct questions
Questions require direction
What is being asked of who?
Who is being asked for what?

Desire dances through ambivalence
I want
Without direct what or who
A hunger without clear definition

A baby crying
For food? Comfort? Change of clothes?
Do they even know?
A felt sense of need
A struggle to pin it down

Pin me down
Reduce the options
Offer me shelter from decision fatigue
Tell me I deserve it
To be met and held in my unknowing

Seasonal Signs

9

Every year
The very early start to Christmas card season
begins
With one card, postmarked from the UK,
Without a full proper return address
Comes mailed to B. Kilgore
Today it arrived
Marking the turning of seasons

Fruiting Bodies

Scar roots reach
Pinch at one end,
Pulls the other

Mycellial in nature
Subsurface networks
Fruiting bodies

Holding it together
Movement across every plane
Scaffold rigidity

B.T.E.

Big top energy
Cheers and roars
On the verge of tears
Biting lip under mask
Do my wet eyes catch the sparkling lights?
Humans riding their mortal edge
A missed step and it's over
Missing the kids step-mom
Who can't be out under the big top
Too close to her own mortal edge

Apples/Trees

12

I stand in the driveway of my father's childhood
home
My daughter is enrapt in play and conversation
with her cousin
Unbreakable conversations a birthright to them
both
I stand on the gravel driveway
Repeating, okay, it's time to go
As I have done my entire life
Our children play under the tree
Heavy with apples
Grafted by our grandfather
The fruit falls at its roots

Death Mother

Always a dead mom story
A new girlfriend, bonded through digital grief
sex over her mother's death bed
Complains at my choice of movies

Never intentionally poking that specific tender
fresh wound
Digital divination, algorithmic curation
Another dead mom story

Story progresses, she becomes a "mom" to mine
Children's stories and cartoons, ancient to
modern
Fairy tale canon is dead mom central

Holy mother
Bless us and keep us
Let your light shine onto us
Goddess worship
The divine creative force
The womb in which everything we know was
cooked in
Mother earth, the salty ocean
Water breaks
Transition to active labour

Full body purge
Every living thing, cursed looking deep water
fish and majestic soaring Eagle
The good, bad, everything in between
It all belongs to the mother
Matriarch

She's been poisoned
Imprisoned
Left to die
Race to a finish line
On the very edge of possible
The scrambling masses seemingly oblivious to
their culpability
Subconsciously returning again and again to the
well of story

Another dead mom story to meet my grief
To speak directly to the disconnect
That is patriarchal consumption
Coughing blood, feeling faint

Another dead mom story to normalize this pain
A collective wound
It's not personal
But deeply intrinsic

Ancient mom stories demonized
Burned at the stake

Recast, a meek and humble virgin
A servant used, not a portal-bearing powerhouse
with agency
A vengeful monster, not a violated and self
protective force
Evil stepmothers always driving the story
toward violence and separation, not offering
comfort and care to a grievous child
Competition.
Pitted against each other
So as to ignore the man behind the curtain

Another dead mom story
Front row seat
Slowly unfolding
Buckle in,
grab some snacks and tissues
This one is personal

Soup

Fog, thick like pea soup
That's what they say right?
Peas porridge hot? Peas porridge cold?
Congealed and rancid in a pot, nine days old?
Getting caught in the fog illustrative of the
problem itself

The overwhelmption.
Predictability? Impossible
The stress.
The hair loss.
The lack of sleep.
Appointment notes scribbled in descending
precision
A feeling of being on call for the next fire
A last minute ride or acquisition mission

Leaning hard on routine
Plans. Collaborations. Body doubles.
Tuning out and going through the motions

Gathering of witches
Across 4 lands
Music begins and I am still caught in the soup
Speaker, talk to phone. Phone, talk to speaker.

No? Fuck. OK. Fine.

Vampire gloves on
Reaching though the soup to feel where I begin
Tracing out the edges
Feeling into it
Grabbing tight and tracing soft leather
backhands
Gloves off, nipple clamps on
Tying a leash to this body i found in the fog
Keeping it secure and within my grip
While I take it to the bath.
Candles.
Fresh water running.
Hot as can be.
Lower the body into the hot water
Firm grip on the leash

The soup melts off.
Flesh feels
Eventually cold
Add more hot
Candle cast shadows of the goddess dance on
the wall
The flesh feels
The body melts

Practice is closing
Witches reconvene

Linger
Add more hot, more times

Come back often.
Especially when the soup is fog thick

Mist Melting

Paddle up the gorge
To the detached
Swim dock, just shy
Of the narrows

The mist & the cold
Have all burned off
The hot skin kisses of
A sun that started elusive
Under layers of knits

Transfixed by the
Shadow reflections on
The leaves, beginning to
orange & brown
Over hanging the rippling water

Rocked gently, the water
A sweet caring parent
Taken me into embrace

The tears come in waves
Other days feel
so deep in a fog
That tears
Vaporize before emerging

Undertow

Intimacies lost gradually
Shared passions stolen
Slipped through days lost
Searching for connection
Where the map has started to tear
Waterlogged with salty brine
Tension in the reach
Time bombs of grief appear unexpected
Thrown back to new love
And forwards past the big goodbye
Whiplashed in the present
Unsure which way is even up anymore

Commitment Prayer

21

I will.
I will pray.
On my knees.
On my back.

I will hold you accountable.
I will offer myself to be held.
I wish to collaborate in sensual desires.
I wish for the electric pleasure of touch.
Sinning vanilla, passion, romance, dominance
Life beyond fear

Hurry Up

Hurry up

            And

                  Wait

Too

            Little

Too

            Late

The next step up is where the answers lie

Lie
Misinformed

Mx. & Ms. Informed regret to inform you, that
your information, has long been in-formation

Tell us something that we don't already know

Don't make it out to be something that it's not

Shoot straight, us queers are already accounting
for the conditions

Urgent waiting lists

Ordering tests

Calls to book appointments that could have been
calls

No calls or notices; missed appointments

5 calls, 2 mailed notices, an email each day;
appointment postponed

Attempts to postpone mortality must be
submitted in writing

Blue Ink, Block Letters, handwritten triplicate

Hurry Up

    And

        Wait

The road sounds wet

24

Each wave of traffic
Churning up stream
Major thoroughfare
Former water way

Daylight creeks
Shopping carts upended
Paved over paradigm
Flooded sealed flood plain

In the forest
wet sounds different
It has places to go
Absorbed and redistributed

Blum

She asks, are you ok? You seem blum
Blum being the made up word our toddler used
after a partial introduction to
glum and bummed
Got jumbled up to make a new word
That describes the melancholy of
disappointment

This coded dialect is dying
As any language does when one third of its
speakers loses fluency through assimilation
Another third dies
And the last remaining third is overcome by
grief

A language with so few remaining speakers
It sits somewhere between critically endangered
and extinct

The commote troll hides under the couch
blankets with a secret stash of balloons
Living off stray fwy bits and susee crumbs

When no longer called by name
Will the troll die too

Or will it find itself transmogrified
Into the mundane household item
That does its job in other homes
Stripped of its magical overlay
Nothing more than circuitry and batteries

I am blum
At witnessing horrendous atrocities across the
world
But also at the knowing that someday soon
I will find myself blum in a context
Where the concept itself is unknown

Calibrate for Distortion

A day to myself
I dive into indexing old note books
Filtering baby clothes and keepsakes
Photo albums and heirloom quilts and afghans

The sort of things that cannot be replaced
A flood, a fire, a bombing
Running for ones life
Or even the big final exit

Left behind
Mostly meaningless to anyone else
Not really incredibly useful on the daily
Archived clues, time travel checkpoints

The artifacts tell a softer version
Than my brains record
Sweeter, kinder, gentler
Diving in to calibrate memory

Defrag regularly enough
Keep conditions from sprouting
Socks growing ears of their own
To hear their own version

All At Once

All at once
Or drawn out over time?

Ancient traditions mandated a period
A grieving year
To stand by the fire
And be held

Now, our world is rapid fire
Back to business, back to normal
Back to numbing and escaping

2 days bereavement leave
Keep it together
Living keep on living
Isolated in the crowd

A break in the chain
Takes time to mend
Rushing in to using something
Undergone loss, not yet settled

Snap. Collapse. Brace.
Shelter in place. Displace.
Erased. Death. Loss. Over.
Empty. Hollow. Numb.

School Girl Crush

Nineteen ninety five
A five way intersection
Five safety vested grade fives
With handheld stop signs
The crushing pressure built over time
Calling out to him by name
Without anything specific to say
Under no circumstances
Admitting, confessing, divulging
Stealing fantasy and throwing it's perfection
Into moving traffic

He stepped forward
Ya?
A bird on the wire above
Shit directly on the spot he had just been
standing
Only divine or profound
As a secret childish crush
Letting the tiniest steam off
Dodging turd in his eternally fresh buzzcut

Two thousand and two
Never really a sports spectator
I found myself tracking track practice

Watching him run
Pubescent rush of the short sprints
Tried baton twirling with the marching band
For some alternative reason
To be frequenting the chip rubber

Two thousand twenty three
Brief appearance at the reunion
Just long enough to chat with each of these now
men
One is a bus driver with an 8 year old who wants
to be a mortician
One works in the city planning office, not here,
and not doing actual progressive planning, but
just one desk over.
Good men? Kind men.
Immediately friendly and not hung up for one
second that I was once a girl that secretly
crushed on them
Not that they could even know the secret part
Now we are all just grown men, talking about
death and parenting and the insanity of the
housing market.